My Wave of Words

A BOOK OF POETRY
BY MARILYN E. PATTON GARCIA

RoseDog Books
PITTSBURGH, PENNSYLVANIA 15222

The contents of this work including, but not limited to, the accuracy of events, people, and places depicted; opinions expressed; permission to use previously published materials included; and any advice given or actions advocated are solely the responsibility of the author, who assumes all liability for said work and indemnifies the publisher against any claims stemming from publication of the work.

All Rights Reserved
Copyright © 2005 by Marilyn E. Garcia
No part of this book may be reproduced or transmitted in any form or by any means, electronic or mechanical, including photocopying, recording, or by any information storage and retrieval system without permission in writing from the author.

ISBN # 0-8059-9853-5
Printed in the United States of America

First Printing

For additional information or to order additional books, please write:
RoseDog Publishing
701 Smithfield Street
Pittsburgh, Pennsylvania 15222
U.S.A.
1-800-834-1803
Or visit our web site and on-line bookstore at
www.rosedogbookstore.com

Dedication

This book is dedicated with the up-most affection and the deepest love to my mom Louise Patton. Her love, wisdom and strength have helped me to become the woman that I am today.

To my daughter Mercedes Garcia who is my inspiration and a dream come true. Mommy loves you and I am so proud to have you as a daughter. To all my nieces, nephews, friends and the rest of my family I love you all.

Contents

Day Dreams... 1
Life 2
The Man 3
That Magic 4
We Dare To Merge 5
Snow 6
The Value Of Money 7
Got The Message 8
Lady O 9
My Love 10
Poetry Is 11
Expressions 12
In Matrimony 13
My Little Girl 14
My Mom 15
When You're Hooked 16
Time 17
He Is 18
To Be Young 19
Abuse 20
The World 21
One Of Those Days 22
My Brother's Keeper 23
So Fine 24
The Other Woman 25
In Memory Of Janice 26
Signs That Let You Know 27
Silence 28
Menace To Society 29
My Rock 30
That Light 31
Our Forgiveness 32
Can I Make A Suggestion? 33
The Soldier Returns 34
The Mexican 35
The Shade Of Sadness 36
Louis H. Pink Houses 37
The First Time 38

Grace	39
Choice Of Weapons	40
Tale Of Two Cities	41
Here I stand	42
A Mirror Image	43
Let's Make Love	44
Relevancy	45
Weather Report	46
The Sound Of Silence	47
Our Thoughts	48
Blind Date	49
Gossip	50
Surviving Disaster	51
Anger	52
What's In A Name	53
Honor	54
What Happened To Love	55
Space	56
Soul	57
Images	58
So Low	59
Rejection	60
Peace	61
The Admirer	62
Disease	63
I Dare You	64
A Kiss	65
Compassion	66
Consequences	67
Caution	68
The Past	69
The Pipe	70
Questions	71
Love Is	72
My Husband	73
My Wife	74
Ms. Thing	75
The Policeman	76

Montel 77
My Father 78
VESTAL 79

Introduction

Marilyn Elizabeth (Patton) Garcia was born on August 12th of 1957 in Brooklyn, New York in the Louis H. Pink Housing Projects. I have been writing poetry since the age of 15. Poetry is my wave of words and allows me to express myself with my point of view on subjects that are important to me. It reflects my opinion on life's challenges. On January of 2005 and December 0f 2003, I received "The Editors Choice Award" for "Outstanding Achievement In Poetry", presented by Poetry.Com and The International Library of Poetry.

I have been writing Poetry for over 30 years. It keeps me grounded and on point. Sometimes it is much better to put your thoughts on paper instead of keeping them all bottled up inside of you. I hope you will enjoy taking a ride with me on my wave of words. This is a collection of some of my favorite poems and hope it brings you pleasure in reading them.

Biography

I attended Clara Barton Vocational High School in Brooklyn New York until 1974. My family and I moved to Cambria Heights, New York and I graduated from Andrew Jackson High School in June of 1976. In 1987 I moved to Upstate New York. I have a beautiful daughter named Mercedes who is my inspiration.

I attended MWBE Development Center Inc. (Minority Women's Business Enterprise) which I completed the Entrepreneurial Assistant Program in the Fall of 2001, to complete my business plan and start my own business.

I received the "New York State Senate Excelsior Award" and a "Certificate Of Special Congressional Recognition" for "Mercedes Clothing & Accessories" (The Clothing Store On Wheels) for "Outstanding And Invaluable Service To The Community," as well as "The BSB Bank & Trust Company" Certificate Of Recognition. I am also a member of Semper Fidelis and the NAACP.

My poem entitled "Life" appears in the book "The Colors Of Life", by "The international Library Of Poetry", and my poem entitled "My Mom" is included in the book "Great Poems Of The Western World by "The Famous Poets Society" which will be released in the Spring of 2005. In addition to writing Poetry, I have also completed a Fictional Novel and three Children's books which I co-wrote with my daughter Mercedes and I will publish in the near future.

For You

Acknowledgment

I would like to thank my mother, Louise Patton for always being there for me through all of my life challenges and for being my rock. You are the epiphany of a woman and you personify what it means to be a good mother. Your support and your commitment to family is something that I have always admired. I love you mother.

I thank my siblings for being my best friends and for not judging each other when we fall short of our shortcomings. We as brothers and sisters have not always agreed upon everything but we stick together as family.

I thank my daughter Mercedes Garcia for being the great little girl she is. That smile and laugh she has brightens my day. You are a terrific kid. You are exceptional, courageous and beautiful. I only hope I can teach you to be independent and all of the values and morals that my mom and dad taught me.

I thank all of my nieces, nephews, aunts, uncles and cousins for being my family. I thank you for your encouragement, your patience and support while I completed this book. To all my friends past and present our friendship has with stood the test of time. You are not only my friends; you are my extended family.

I thank my sister-in-law Lynda Patton for all of her help throughout the years. Any problems I have had you were always there for me. I love you and I hope each and every one of you knows that I will always be here in mind as well as in spirit.

Day Dreams

A mystical creation of the imagination.

Can be on occasion seemingly frustrating.

Can keep you in leaps at the edge of your seats.

Can be very complicated.

If you awake by the edge of a stake

Then your dream must have seem frightfully pleasing.

© 2004

Life

Most of the time it had me aggravated and humiliated.

How could life get anymore complicated?

Do I get agitated or intimidated?

What is life suppose to teach?

Do I continue to preach?

I should have reached.

Why didn't I hear my screams?

Realize my own damn dreams.

What should I have said or done?

If only I had heard a promising word.

The forceful and sometime demanding voice was my own.

© 2004

The Man

Courteous to others at all times.
Loving and loyal and he's all mine.
Ambitious and always focused.
Reliable on your worst day.
Exciting and street educated.
Never gets intimidated in any way.
Charming and dedicated.
Excellent communicator and greatly appreciated.

© 2004

That Magic

A carriage ride through Central Park.

That magic

Those long distant talks on the phone in which you express he is above all the rest.

That magic

A blazing fire on a cold night, he takes you in his arms and holds you tight.

That magic

Riding horses through a meadow

That magic

Waiting three months to make love to that special someone

That magic

Sharing your hopes and dreams for the future you share.

That magic.

Knowing how much he really does care.

That magic

Your child graduating and finally leaving home

That magic

Thanking god she had the good sense not to stray or roam.

That magic

© 2004

We Dare to Merge

Okay, he had the almost fully paid for condo.

You had your fully furnished townhouse, which you will be paying for forever.

Okay, he had the ultimate fireplace.

You have the black leather sofa to sit on.

Okay, he has a beautiful Vincent illustration.

You have a brass and glass picture of horses, which you cherish and he wishes you would relinquish.

Okay he has the raised, four post bed with the comfortable mattress.

You have the black lace negligee, which he takes off to his satisfaction.

Okay he has the warm, loving, comforting arms.

You have had enough and can no longer resist his charms.

© 2004

Snow

Ice crystals formed directly from water vapor.

In another form an addiction, which does not discriminate.

It can segregate, humiliate and most surely separate you from yourself.

It can call you back and talk to you on any given night.

Come over, come over, come over here and get a light.

It can bring you down, down, down.

It can leave you friendless.

Make you feel emotionally endless.

But rest assured you can always be lured back to that state of emptiness

© 2004

The Value of Money

It has a distinction.

What is socially real and what is fiction?

It offers a reaction.

And sometimes not welcome attraction.

When you had some, it left you in amazement.

And oh! How we sometimes do waste it.

Some people get caught up in it.

The thought of what can be bought and sold with it.

© 2004

Got the Message

Communicating in writing, by speaking or signal has definitely ended.
Comprehension has begun by fighting, yelling or screaming which now has a new meaning.
You have tried to break all ties.
Now here comes some more lies.
Will he ever accept that it is over?
When I said that we were through
You pretended like you did not have a clue.
All I want to be now is left alone.
My feelings are hurt by the nasty messages you left on my phone.
Don't beg for forgiveness because you have already lost me.
I hope you get the message there is no more we.

© 2004

Lady O

Oh what we are seeing that fabulous human being.

Such style, such grace that incredible face.

Thousands of TV viewers watch that down to earth beauty.

The millions of quest on her show can't get enough of her glow.

All blessings, all praises are made

To the woman who gave to thousands of charities.

She has donated millions with such clarity.

Keep up the good will.

So many hearts you do fill.

That woman we all love from the heavens above.

All praises to Oprah Winfrey.

© 2004

My Love

Loving you has been an art form.

There was no need for structure.

Never a need to conform

This realism we share.

So precious, so rare

Cannot be compared.

In all of my days

In multiple ways

I will always love you.

As we keep flourishing

Our love still nourishing

© 2004

Poetry Is

An explosion of lyrics that trickles down paper

The most satisfying mind blowing classics.

The most interesting topics

It is a stroll down memory lane.

So much incite to gain.

Not only a walk through life.

But it is meant to excite.

It is a calm peaceful wave.

Keeps each reader enslaved.

It brings me to a conclusion.

It transforms my world into an illusion.

© 2004

Expressions

Sometimes a lethal weapon of emotions

From the rolling of the eyes or the half cocky looks of disbelieve.

Sometimes a jungle of circumstances hidden in your smile or grin

From the look of embarrassment as shock splatters itself all over your face.

Sometimes able to read and more often then never preconceived.

The look of love or the feeling of hurt we cannot frown upon the roads our faces take to so many places.

© 2004

In Matrimony

You thought it would be spending your life with your best friend.

You were hoping this right up to the end.

That guy you knew that you loved.

Only he turned out to be a thug.

This shattered all of your hopes and dreams.

This made you mad it made you scream.

The knock on the door and you on the floor

Next thing that you knew this couldn't be you.

Now as you look back and see.

Wow was that really me?

Now that you are reconstructed and fully conscious

Of all your misconceptions

He begs for your forgiveness for all of his indiscretions.

© 2004

My Little Girl

What a jewel, What a Pearl.

That best describes my little girl.

Such a gem and oh so slim

She possesses that knowledge.

She will do well in college.

Quick to elate

She has my traits.

Through life's joys and sorrows

She still has tomorrow.

What we have learned

From that child we discern

By the knowledge so relevant

By the child who is prevalent

© 2004

My Mom

Imagine an earthquake, ground splitting.
She is the cement that puts it all back together.
Imagine experiencing turbulence on an airplane.
She is a parallel or vertical line.
Imagine thunder and lightening, which is so frightening.
She is my sunshine on a rainy day.
Imagine a heat wave or sunstroke.
She is the air conditioning in a doctor's office, which we all wonder why is it up so high?
Imagine having a temperature, which you were always told, take some Tylenol.
She is camomile tea, honey, with a twist of lemon.
Imagine educating a (A) student in Princeton University.
She has no documented degree.
She is the epiphany of what a woman is suppose to be.
You personify what the word mother means to me.
Imagine someone who would always offer comforting arms.
Now you can imagine my mom?

© 2004

When You're Hooked

The sale at Macy's said Take Off 75% and 100% of your credit card is already spent.

You have 15 pairs of the same shoes in Tan but you still need pecan.

You right a check knowing there is nothing in your bank account growing.

You have already called him 25 times and he hasn't returned any of your calls.

You say to yourself he's got some balls.

You have gambled away the family fortune at the casino.

You say to yourself "just one more spin"; I know I can win.

You have spent the last 22 hours watching HSC.

Your brand new car is being repossess by the bank.

© 2004

Time

We watch it and we wait for it.

We depend on it and we abuse it.

We see it and we feel it.

We need it to succeed in it.

We rush it and we make it.

We live in it and wait to die in it.

It stops for no one.

It waits on no one.

© 2004

He Is

He is a gentle breeze that blows softly onto me.

His touch softens and caresses my skin.

He is the best of me whole heartily within.

He is the river that flows over me.

He inhabits me.

His love drives me crazy.

His knowledge empowers me.

His is the love that will devour me.

He is precise in his interpretation of me.

His love takes my breath away.

© 2004

To Be Young

When you are young, you think you know all the answers.
You're mom might say, "Stay in school" and don't spread your legs.
If I knew then what I know now, maybe I could afford to feed my child.
I didn't wait until I was wed before I let him share my bed.
Now I sit and ponder, how do I care for this small wonder?

© 2004

Abuse

You thought you could handle it.

His love was entanglement.

Consumed with the need to hear you scream

He shattered all your hopes and dreams.

All that you shared in your desperate despair

Now is all over, for one moment, you once thought he cared.

© 2004

The World

In society's world we take a twirl.

We can therefore appreciate the things that are inanimate.

In these trying times of need, something is always perceived.

If we have truly learned from life's lessons that we were taught

We can therefore achieve without all the greed.

© 2004

One of Those Days

The alarm clock does not go off at 7:30 but you think it is still early.
The car in your path has suddenly run out of gas.
The friend that you trusted has just gotten you busted.
The child that you cherished has suddenly perished.
You're significant other has slept with your brother.
You've just heard a shot and you're homey was popped.

© 2004

My Brothers Keeper

I have seen Heroine have him kneeling.

When ordinarily he would have been competing.

I've seen it put him in such despair.

His wasted life in much needed repair.

I've seen it let me know he needs me.

When others won't even feed him.

The joy of love and hope perceives me.

I still remember the day it was over.

The drops of rain the smell of clover.

© 2004

So Fine

You thought he was so fine.

He finally unlocked his mind.

His mission in life was to explore more and more.

Who else other than you, he could sleep with once more.

If all had not been said and done

You were tested HIV positive

Who could conceive in your moment to grieve?

That now you find out your pregnant and that everything else is irrelevant.

© 2004

The Other Woman

When the first call came you never suspected.
Your feelings and emotions were never protected.
The lovable man you thought you knew.
Has always been cheating on you.
And if you thought that this is the worst it could get.
His wife calls you up with some bodily threats.

© 2004

In Memory of Janice

She stood 5ft. 4" and her skin was high yella.

She was misunderstood and she couldn't endure what life had in-store for her.

She devoted her time to heroine, cheap tricks and wine.

In remembrance of my friend and the life she once dreamed of.

Without malice I offer my love and this poem to Janice.

© 2004

Signs That Let You Know

Car payment is due he now has the flu.

Notes payable is payable and he is suddenly disabled.

He is missing in action.

He is always distracted.

Your time together is not equivalent.

You are no longer relevant.

The relationship you structured

Contains nothing but punctures.

When he is away it is just another day.

© 2004

Silence

That sound we never hear.
It sounds all so clear.
If at that instance it had not been spoken.
The silence you seek was considered a mere token.
You would have not heard any conversation.
The peace that you wanted was just a revelation.
Talking wasn't relevant and certainly not prevalent.
No need to hear. Silence is near.

© 2004

Menace to Society

He might be your neighbor his demeanor is smug.

That rude and rambunctious teen

That around-the-way thug

His look so sinister and mean

Who would have thought

He could never be taught.

He is not hesitant in his explorations.

He is right up front with all his manipulations.

© 2004

My Rock

It is strong, firm and hard.

It can penetrate my heart.

It releases things in all of us.

It is subject to roll or fall.

It can move back and forth

It has rhythm that you can hear through walls.

It is sometimes thrown or picked up.

It is also something that can be cooked up.

It is also a form of candy and sometimes comes in very handy.

© 2004

That Light

It shines so very bright.

It gives us the ability to see the light.

It flares, it glares and it sometimes snares.

It ascends, it mends and it sometimes even pretends.

It captures and it raptures.

It motivates and appreciates.

That beam with the gleam

Oh! What does it really mean?

© 2004

Our Forgiveness

That very same friend that you thought you had
He is the very same one who just shot your dad.
We offer our forgiveness.
Although our child has suffered immensely you and I continue to fight over custody.
We offer our forgiveness.
Our perfect marriage has been destroyed; by the same woman you have been seeing in Detroit.
We offer our forgiveness.
As we finally get home and open our premises everything we own seems to be missing.
We offer our forgiveness.
Our Harvard bound son has just been shot with the very same gun that you just got.
We offer our forgiveness.

© 2004

Can I Make A Suggestion

Not far from my home which is in mint condition

There is my home girl's house, which is filthy beyond recognition.

Can I make a suggestion

The night your evening shift got started

You decided to go out and party.

Can I make a suggestion

You decided to tell your best friends old man

That she has been whoring around with some other man.

Can I make a suggestion

You quit your job without having another one in place

Now you're a member of the unemployed rat race.

Can I make a suggestion

© 2004

The Soldier Returns

With baggage in hand he returns to the land of the brave and the home of the free.

As he opens his bedroom door he cannot ignore what his heart has endured.

Too much of his surprise there on his bed lies his wife and his next-door neighbor.

The women he wed had someone else in his bed.

Well after the fight and regaining his sight he so needed to remember.

Not far from the past our relationships don't last as well as our hopes and dreams for the future.

© 2004

The Mexican

He is tall, olive complexion and has the look of perfection.

To my surprise underneath those green eyes and that skin, lay someone more sinister.

There was never any question when I made my selection that he would one day be mine.

Through the black eyes and bruises I still couldn't walk away.

Through the years and my tears I still couldn't figure why I stayed.

Ten years later as we sit across the table, he still has that flavor and an even more sinister grin.

© 2004

The Shade of Sadness

Just plain black day

Never a light

No where in sight

I don't have a clue

What next I should do

With all of my sorrows

The not promised tomorrows

As I look for some sign

I've recaptured my mind

I have hope for the near future.

© 2004

Louis H. Pink Houses

It could never be measured
My moments of pleasure
Back at Louis H. Pink
To the urine smelling halls
To the neighbors with balls
I give all praise
To the child that you raised
The life lessons I learned
The family structure so firm
I give you this gift
With much sentiment
Keep standing, keep landing

© 2004

The First Time

Too much of my delight, I thought that special night
Would be filled with intimacy and you could be trusted.
This person I knew only made me blue and feel so disgusting.
When all the facts were in, "She slept with all my friends"
This was the news I heard around the clock.
In my school and at the market I was the target.
That was the message you sent around every block.

© 2004

Grace

Lord help me to face
That sometimes difficult place
Show me the inner most meaning
Of what I am feeling
Let me know where I must go
Allow me my space
To educate the human race
The things our minds hold will help us to mold
Much brighter stars for the future

© 2004

Choice of Weapons

Should you aim with a gun or consider your son.

Do you cut with a blade or wait for the anger to fade.

Think about the mistakes you have already made.

Do you wholly in doubt what the fight was really about.

Did you consider what would have happened if you let him live.

You would still have tomorrow instead of that 25 to life bid.

© 2004

Tales of Two Cities

Your need to escape sometimes take you to that state of mind.
Thinking your in France when Brooklyn is really within your grasp.
That place which you have always known should be considered your permanent home.
But just as it was a dream that special place really seemed so far away.
And if by chance you take a glance back into reality.
You will see that the home you've known is merely a technicality.

© 2004

Here I Stand

Against the wall and so appalled.
For that which was intended
Has now been rescinded.
You could not depend on it.
What is now known as factuality
Is just really a technicality
Please don't misbelieve my sincerity
And stop and accept my apologies.

© 2004

A Mirror Image

So you are at the 50 yd. line of life's scrimmage.

You can finally recognize that mirror image.

That motherly need to protect and to shield

The child you are losing and you cannot yield.

Whether their lies are fictional or factual the truth remains actual

Me loving you and you loving me

I never judged you and please don't judge me.

This bond that we share can never compare

This love that I hold for my child that I mold

Please accept my apologizes

For all the times I had to scold you.

© 2004

Let's Make Love

He entered me and it was all over
That feeling of warmth with my beautiful lover
That need for us to reach our sexual peak
There's no need to ponder my sensual wonder.
Who knew through the rapture
A sensational love would be captured.

© 2004

Relevancy

The things that we hold to be relevant
Can not compare to what is prevalent
Our need to succeed
Not selfishness, nor greed
The things we concern ourselves with
The peoples lives that are destroyed by it
When will we ever finally come together?

© 2004

Weather Report

The sun rises and sets

The rain pours and it's wet

The wind blows and twirls in devastation

The earth, what a perceptive sensation

© 2004

The Sound of Silence

To refrain from hearing noise though just a sound

Too much of it can cause extreme depression.

It should be left to your discretion.

That moment of silence we seek

Nowhere to be found and all too meek

That time that we treasure one moment of pleasure.

© 2004

Our Thoughts

Did I hear you knock?

Find the right key to unlock

We all have that gift

When left unscathed

It gives us a lift

It help us to know

Where we are going

© 2004

Blind Date

It's mystical and magical
It's down right infallible
Although it may seem
This must be a dream
Though friends initiated it
It was greatly appreciated

© 2004

Gossip

Sometimes fatal and rest assuredly labeled.
No one will refrain from
There's much loss and no gain
You sit and procrastinate
Do you tell or just wait?
And if it is told who gets hurt
By you spilling that unnecessary dirt

© 2004

Surviving Disaster

With all of life's ups and downs you take what you can

With the hope the rest of your stuff will still be around

Do we grieve or adhere to those treasures we hold dear?

To whose admission can we draw a conclusion?

Or perhaps this was just an illusion.

The immensity of its complexity

Leaves you feeling such heartache.

The possessions you left behind which you couldn't take.

Let us hope and let us prey

That you and your neighbors will see another day

© 2004

Anger

It is the strongest feeling of displeasure.

By what means could it possibly be measured?

Although acts of deceit and never discrete.

It is all so frustrating and a feeling of destitute.

Even those so call friends we now hate.

The perception we thought we could naturally inarticulate.

Through that destructive realism beams feeling of distinctiveness.

Although closure is near, we seem to never adhere.

© 2004

What's in a Name?

That single and sometimes unpopular name you are called.

No matter what it is, it sometimes leaves you feeling disgraced and rest assuredly appalled.

You often sit and ponder how people can be so conjuring.

Do they get their kicks from the pain you are enduring?

No sense of consequence and their lacking common sense.

© 2004

Honor

High regard or respect for that individual with mass intellect.
We try to intermingle and socialize
The same people who offer you critiquing.
Never the respect that you were seeking.
All to eminent and never prevalent to what we hold as relevant.

© 2004

What Happened to Love?

The deepest affection no needed protection.
That space in your heart you never disregard.
Sometimes shielded never to be yielded.
Once upon a time it was certainly enchanting.
Now left abruptly broken and taken for granted.

© 2004

Space

That area of a room or time you choose not to be confined.
The level of comfort you wish could be confronted.
If time could elapse your hindered past
Hopefully one day you will find some peace at last.

© 2004

Soul

The nature of man whether spiritual or emotional

The depths of us all as caring individuals

Never to be inhibited by life's changes

The love of us all as human beings

Can never be limited and has such a vital meaning.

© 2004

Images

A reflection of someone we thought we knew.
Could this be me or was that you?
Does that face have a look of disgrace?
It captures so many emotions and expressions.
If left neglected it can't be protected.

© 2004

So Low

Things couldn't get any worse

That's what you thought.

Not knowing which way to turn next

What help can be sought?

I should have done this

Why didn't I do that?

That endless feeling you sometimes get

You've reached rock bottom

So now what's next?

The answer not found in any text

Waiting around hopelessly with so much regret

© 2004

Rejection

Sometimes in life we are left feeling array.

You wanted him and suddenly

You were left feeling empty

Was I not good enough just being me?

The talents I possess you just couldn't see.

My feelings and emotions were never considered.

Now I sit and ponder

What the hell was your problem?

I know I am a woman

A Head strong and magnificent wonder.

© 2004

Peace

Do you think I can have some?
Mentally, physically, emotionally and spiritually
Being of both sound mind and body
Never hoping to run across the obvious phonies
Let me have my space
Please don't reject me because of my race
My inner well being is much too meaningful to me
I hope one day that you to can see it

© 2004

The Admirer

Can I put you in a jar and watch you from afar?
I sometimes reveal the secret things I feel.
Obsession and sometimes possession are shown to my discretion.
Should I let you know that you are a blessing?
Could I get anymore closer to you without trespassing?
Hovering over you would lead eventually to smothering you.
Do I just sit back and watch hoping never to get caught.
Should I just tell you, you are in all of my thoughts.

© 2004

Disease

It takes it form as weakness
That all too familiar bleakness
It's shapes vary in sizes of all kind
It grows it flows and it nourishes
The young, the old and the people we cherish
It penetrates through bone
It hovers around corners
Affecting the graceful and elaborate
The very much appreciated
It watches and it waits hoping one day to designate
The gifted and dearly loved
Will one day be sent above

© 2004

I Dare You

I dare you to dream.

I dare you to scream.

I dare you to ponder.

I dare you to wonder.

I dare you to give.

I dare you to live.

I dare you to respect.

I dare you to protect.

I dare you to know.

I dare you to grow.

© 2004

A Kiss

To touch without protection
An act of affection
The meeting of two lips
Not sure who has been kissed
That intimate place we put our face
Oh rest assured you can be lured
It nestles and sometimes restricts
Those seemingly safe individuals
We sometimes give a kiss
Although you don't know
Which way this could go
Does it mean what it seems?
Or is it just a conflict of interest?

© 2004

Compassion

We share this gift the need to uplift.
That feeling so treasured and never measured.
Show some emotion and the greatest devotion.
We don't have to understand
Those complex things that make you a man
Feel the need to succeed without all the greed.

© 2004

Consequences

You knew when you did it
You would get some reaction
What were you thinking?
You couldn't retract it.
Although you knew
It would consume you
Bring anger to the people around you
If only you could take it back
Make up for the knowledge
You seem to lack
You probably would have seen
What you did was horrid and mean

© 2004

Caution

Let us proceed with care and knowledge

You are being challenged

To see if you can manage

So lets see just what you can endure

The things not planned

The things you are not sure of

Be hesitant with your approach

When it is all said and done

You will be the one

Who did not resist

Temptation at its best

If it was left up to you

Please remember what you should do.

© 2004

The Past

When you look back now
Why didn't you know?
Why didn't you realize?
Why didn't you grow from it?
Didn't you mean to achieve
Why do you still grieve
All those dreams you thought of.
It has contributed in part
Where you are today
It has shown you a different way
It has made you stronger
A fool you are no longer
Now you are securely allure
No matter what pain you had to endure
Do not question what was done is the past
It has certainly taught you a lesson at last.

© 2004

The Pipe

Who would have ever knew

It keeps me feeling blue

I looked by the door

The hit is on the floor

I thought I had some more

It left me abandon

My possessions left stranded

It took away my life

That hit from the pipe

It took away all my dreams

All I hear now are my screams

© 2004

Questions

That puzzling session
You are asked for a decision.
Did I do it, could I do it, should I do it?
I thought I knew it
Some how I blew it
So what is the answer
It feels like some form of Cancer
That eats away at you
Sometimes it will dismay you

© 2003

Love Is

Love is a cool breeze upon my face.
It emotionally takes me to that special place.
It captures me; it raptures me.
It sometimes almost fractures me.
It can be a gentle kiss or a sensual touch.
You should never have to ask for much.
So please be kind when you have my feelings in mind.
Cherish us and please relish me.
That day will come when you relinquish we.

© 2004

My Husband

I never expected to feel so protected by my eternal date.

I never knew that he would be true and he is my soul mate.

I have never had to ask, "Could you cut the grass", or to finish any task.

It never has to be suggested that his paycheck be sequestered.

It is amazing to me that he will always be my king and I his queen.

© 2004

My Wife

Who knew she would be so special to me?
A mother and scholar whose love makes me holler.
She is essence and grace and, "Oh" what a face.
It never seemed that I would find my queen.
All my hopes and dreams have now been redeemed.
At last I have found my soul mate.

© 2004

Ms Thing

She walks around town always fooling around.

She is thin and trim and has the cutest grin.

She knows when she passes that other girls trash her.

She wants special recognition for her bodily condition.

She is lost to the streets and had sex with all the boys she meets.

She was one-of-a-kind until the day her nude body was found.

© 2004

The Policeman

His demeanor is smug although he has never fired his gun.
You would never know what to expect but he will always protect.
He has a passion for life and is just as capable with a knife.
I would never suggest going up against him at will.
Break the law his black belt in karate has the capacity to kill.
Who is this beautiful black man who is a force of one?
His name is Gilbert Pew and he is Ms. Hattie's son.

© 2004

Montel

The marines he did serve

His life was preserved

That bald striking individual

With all that residual

Not lost to MS

The one you should never dismiss

He is a giant and the one who will triumph

He is giving of his knowledge

A brother to be acknowledge

You have the gift

You give a mental lift

To all those around you

Greatness will always surround you

© 2004

My Father

He was born on the 24th of May, had a voice of satin.

So smooth and all so cool, don't ever break his household rules.

Know your place as my child he would say.

Break my rules you will never see another day.

He was married to the kind of woman, who did everything to please him.

She cooked, cleaned and did everything to appease him.

When you stayed out late we had no food on our plates.

He couldn't be trusted and cheated with the woman he lusted.

We still had respect for you although we were neglected.

It was mother who enforced the rules and kept our family protected.

© 2004

Vestal

Vestal is a place unlike no another.

The air is crisp, it's foliage, a magnificent wonder.

It has rolling hills and streets so clean.

I now know what complacency really means.

At that first glance, it will win you over.

That smell of lavender, the four leaf clovers.

The people here are so content.

My neighbors have never shown resentment.

I never thought when I first sought my final resting place.

I would find, a more kinder town and at last have my space.

There are excellent schools and here the seniors rule.

So if by chance you happen to glance at Vestal on the map.

Unlike the City, this town is pretty and you can get here in a snap.

© 2005

JUL 1 4 2006

811 Garcia

Garcia, Marilyn E.
Patton, 1957-
My wave of words : a
book of poetry /
c2005. (A2

JUL 1 4 2006

NO LONGER PROPERTY OF
THE QUEENS LIBRARY.
SALE OF THIS ITEM
SUPPORTED THE LIBRARY.

Queens Library

**Summer Reading
at Queens Library**
Kids and teens who
read during the
summer do better in
school.

Summer Reading is
fun, it's free.
Call 1-718-990-0700
for information.

www.queenslibrary.org